CREATE YOUR OWN

TREASURE HUNT

15+ CIPHERS AND A COMPLETE GUIDE FOR A BUDGET FREE TEAM-BUILDING

MARTIN MORNÁR

Design by Ondrej Sova

Edited by Hazel Miller

ISBN: 978-80-570-6310-0

ACKNOWLEDGMENTS

I owe a huge thank you to everyone who's helped make this book a reality.

First, to the summer camps of my childhood, where I first discovered treasure hunts. Those camp games sparked a fascination that's stayed with me ever since, making every summer feel like an adventure.

A big shoutout to my good friend Nero, who brought treasure hunts from those summer days into our grown-up lives. Nero, you've somehow made every occasion—from birthdays to just-because weekends—a treasure hunt, keeping the spirit alive all these years.

To my colleagues at Slido and Cisco, thank you for your endless enthusiasm for my games. Every Christmas, you made my treasure hunts a highlight of the party. Your encouragement gave me the push to bring this project to life.

And to my amazing wife, Lenka. Thank you for standing by me through every bit of doubt, and for giving me honest, valuable feedback as my favourite playtester.

To all of you, I couldn't have done this without your support and encouragement. Thank you for being a part of the journey!

CONTENTS

ABOUT THE AUTHOR

Hello there! If you're reading this publication, chances are you share my passion for games and the excitement they bring. Ever since I was a kid, I've enjoyed games and the rush of being fully present in the moment.

Over the years, I've had the incredible opportunity to channel my passion into action by organising numerous summer camps for kids and facilitating team-building activities in professional settings, including companies like Slido and Cisco. This is where I truly come alive. It's not just about the fun, although that's certainly a big part of it, but also about the invaluable learning experiences that come from playing, collaborating, creating a strategy and executing plans, all while having a blast and easily learning from along the way. I firmly believe that effective team-building goes beyond improving professional performance; it's about creating trust, memories, and bonds that extend past the office walls.

With this publication I want to share the knowledge and experience I've gathered over the years to help others organise unforgettable experiences with minimal resources and budget. My goal is to provide you with an easy to follow manual that empowers you to create your own treasure hunts and craft unforgettable memories.

Here's to the adventure ahead!

INTRODUCTION

If you've ever felt the rush of excitement that comes from unravelling mysteries, if you're into solving puzzles and escape rooms, then you're in the right place. You're about to enter a thrilling world of creating and experiencing treasure hunts like never before.

A treasure hunt is an amazing game in itself, that works in just about any setting, but it truly shines in an office environment, especially as part of a team-building activity. A treasure hunt combines all the right elements: logic, collaboration, communication, a unique trinity that encourages you to see things from different perspectives and—most importantly—it creates lasting memories with the people you work with. It's the perfect recipe for strengthening relationships both at work and beyond.

In today's challenging times, many companies are tightening their budgets for team activities, making it increasingly difficult to find ways to keep your teams engaged and to have some fun together. This can be frustrating when you want to bring your team closer and create shared experiences. While it's easy to hire an agency or pay for a professionally designed program, a limited budget doesn't mean you have to miss out on a fantastic team-building experience. The best part? You can create a treasure hunt on your own, without breaking the bank! With a little time and dedication, you can craft an engaging treasure hunt that costs next to nothing. This guide is here to help you do just that—plan your very own treasure hunt with minimal to no expenses.

Now, I won't lie to you: putting together a treasure hunt of any size or scale does take some time, possibly over 8 hours to be fair. So, if you're in a rush and need something for tomorrow, you might want to consider a different activity. But here's the thing—every time I create a treasure hunt, what starts as a lengthy task turns into a lot of fun. Before I know it, the time flies by, and I've got a game ready to go. I'm confident you'll have a blast creating yours too!

In this book, I will be focusing on creating treasure hunts for office environments as well as games for virtual teams. With a little creativity, you can easily adapt these tips to other situations—whether it's a retreat, a company birthday, a Christmas party, a school event, or any other gathering where you want to add some excitement.

Another big plus? Treasure hunts are super flexible. You can scale them up from a small game for 10 people to an epic adventure for hundreds. But before we start creating one, here's a clear explanation of the difference between a treasure hunt and another popular game, a scavenger hunt:

A **scavenger hunt** is a game where participants are tasked with finding specific items or completing predefined tasks listed by the organisers. These tasks could include taking photographs (Take a selfie with a CEO or highest-ranking supervisor), counting objects (how many exit signs are there on office floor 8?), or performing creative challenges (Recreate a popular Instagram reel and upload it online using #CompanyScavengerHunt tag). Participants typically work in teams, aiming to be the first to complete the list or to complete the most items on it. While scavenger hunts are very enjoyable, they often lack a clear sense of progress, as participants may not know how well they're doing until the end.

A **treasure hunt** is a game that involves following a series of clues to find a hidden object or prize in a particular order. Instead of a list of tasks, participants are presented with riddles provided by the organiser. These riddles may be encoded using different ciphers (from the simple Caesar cipher to elaborate multi-layer ciphers), requiring participants to decipher the riddle to progress to the next step. Unlike scavenger hunts, where tasks may feel disconnected, treasure hunts offer a clear sense of progression as each clue leads to the next one, bringing participants closer to the treasure and creating an engaging and immersive experience. The key difference lies in the way participants progress through the game. Scavenger hunts focus on completing a number of predefined tasks from a list in no specific order, while treasure hunts challenge participants to become like Indiana Jones, decoding clues and riddles to uncover hidden treasure.

I'm not saying one game is better than the other. I just want to clear up the confusion, as people often mix up the terms. Since this publication is all about riddles and clues, we'll be focusing on treasure hunts. If you're interested in scavenger hunts, stay tuned for my upcoming guides which I'll dive into later.

Now that we're on the same page, a word of caution: This book is designed specifically for beginners. It is not intended for seasoned treasure hunters who participate in riddle-solving events, whether as participants or organisers. Instead, it is aimed at those who are eager to create their first treasure hunt but don't know where to start.

In the pages that follow, you'll start a journey with 15 unique ciphers. At the start of each chapter, you'll have the opportunity to step into the shoes of a participant, trying to solve a new cipher on your own. This hands-on experience allows you to gauge the difficulty level firsthand, offering you insights into what your own participants will encounter on game day. Whether you decide to solve the cipher on your own or not (I recommend you give it a try), each chapter reveals the mechanisms behind the riddle, presents various cipher variants, and provides a detailed, step-by-step guide to crafting your own.

By the time you've conquered these initial 15 chapters, you'll possess the skills and insights needed to create your own ciphers, unlocking a world of endless possibilities. But the manual doesn't end there. We'll delve into the practicalities of preparing your own treasure hunt, exploring the nuances of hosting in both virtual and physical spaces. From the initial stages of preparation to the thrill of game day, we'll cover everything you need to know, including essential materials, timing considerations, effective communication strategies and best practices.

I've been designing these treasure hunts as a yearly team-building highlight for the Christmas Party at Slido's company HQ for almost a decade. While participation has always been optional, we've consistently attracted 50 to 90 players (50-70% attendance) from various teams and regions. The primary goal was always to have fun, and I encouraged teams to include members from different departments, allowing people to get to know each other better in an informal yet structured way.

This guide will show you how to create this game on your own and scale it from a small activity for a single team into a company-wide event. Best of all, you can achieve this with a minimal budget, relying on your creativity, time, and a bit of strategic planning.

So, let the game begin.

CHAPTER 1
THE TEXT BLOCK CIPHER

<pre>
T R E V O C S
H M E X U L I
E B G N I E D
N O R M T H O
E U O O E T T
X R G M E N O
T C L U E I G
</pre>

CAN YOU TRY SOLVING THIS CIPHER ON YOUR OWN?

The text block cipher may seem difficult at first glance, and that's the point! Initially, it appears as a jumble of seemingly random letters arranged within a simple square. You might approach it like a word search puzzle. The more you examine it, the more likely you are to uncover fragments of the solution or even complete words. However, despite these discoveries, the complete solution still needs to be discovered.

The key to unlocking the text block cipher lies in deciphering its reading pattern. In this particular case, the message reveals itself when read from the bottom right corner, spiralling counterclockwise towards the centre.

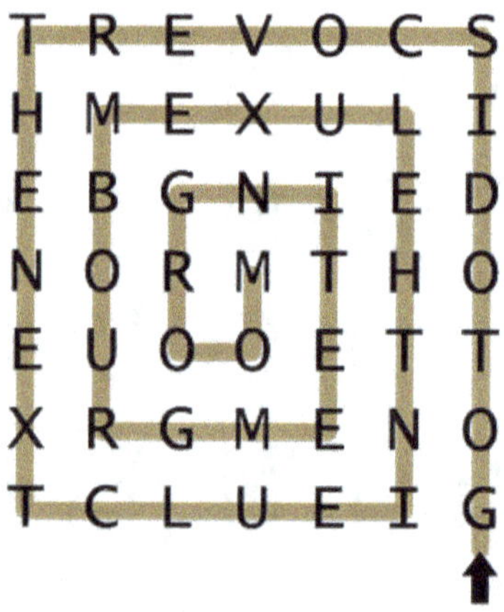

Following this method, you'll eventually uncover the hidden message: **"Go to discover the next clue in the Luxembourg meeting room."**

If your treasure hunt takes place in an office setting, the solution "Luxembourg meeting room" precisely directs the players to the exact location where they should search for the next clue. Precision is crucial; any ambiguity can disrupt the momentum of the game and lead to doubts about whether the solution was deciphered correctly. Participants should encounter no hesitation as they decode the cipher. Clear instructions accelerate their progress, infusing them with a dopamine rush as they successfully unravel the riddle and promptly understand where to look next.

When using the text block cipher, there are several variations to consider. Begin by selecting the number of letters you wish to encrypt. Ideally, your message should fill a square box. For instance, a 5x5 square requires 25 letters, a 6x6 grid requires 36 letters, etc. If these combinations prove unsuitable or if crafting a message within these parameters proves overly challenging, you may opt for a rectangle with dimensions such as 6x5 (30 letters) or 7x6 (42 letters). Should these options still feel restrictive, you can add an exclamation mark or a question mark to the end of the sentence to meet the character limit or simply leave a blank space.

Once you've settled on your message and determined the dimensions, the next step is to choose an encryption path. There are numerous pathing possibilities and variants to consider, ranging from straightforward to more complex options. You can find some examples here.

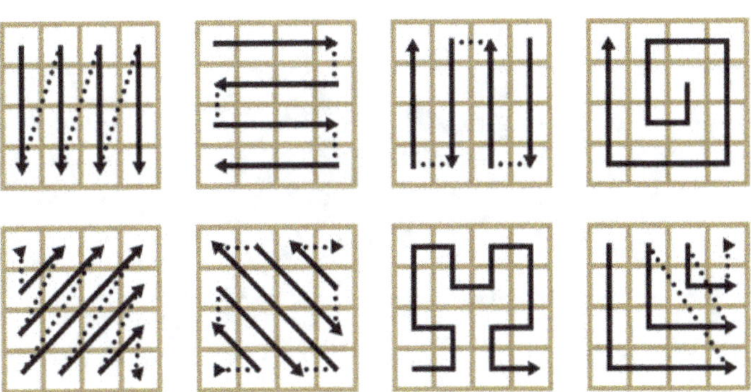

After creating your own text block cipher, it's essential to have someone test it. When you're already familiar with the solution and have encrypted the message yourself, it's easy to underestimate its difficulty. What may appear straightforward to you could pose a significant challenge to others. Therefore, ensure that someone who will not participate on the day tests your cipher. This will provide valuable insight into the level of difficulty of the cipher you've created and how long it might take to solve it during the event.

CHAPTER 2
THE MAZE

CAN YOU TRY SOLVING THIS CIPHER ON YOUR OWN?

The maze presents itself as a visual puzzle. Like any conventional maze, it features a singular entrance and exit. This particular maze, however, lacks dead ends, making navigation straightforward. The true challenge lies in deciphering the purpose of the maze—it is neither an office floor plan nor a complex game of Minesweeper. Counting the tiles available from start to finish reveals precisely 26 tiles, a number that sparks intrigue. Why 26? Well, how many letters does the English alphabet possess? That's right, 26! Coincidence? I think not.

Upon filling the maze with alphabetical letters and following the designated path, every letter is utilised. A few highlighted tiles catch the eye, hinting at their potential significance. The real excitement begins when these highlighted letters are rearranged. The culmination of this rearrangement yields a final answer: A C K L S → SLACK.

This exact cipher was used during my own creation of a treasure hunt for Slido's Christmas Team-building event. The resulting solution seamlessly guided participants into Slack, the main communication platform of the company. Within Slack, they found the public channel called "Treasure Hunt 2024," which contained another clue (I have created the Slack channel on the day of the hunt to prevent people from finding the channel by accident).

This method isn't limited to digital platforms like Microsoft Teams, Yammer, and Discord. It can also guide adventurers to real-world places, making the experience even more diverse and exciting.

Let's explore another example of this cipher, demonstrating its capacity to communicate more complex messages while keeping them concise.

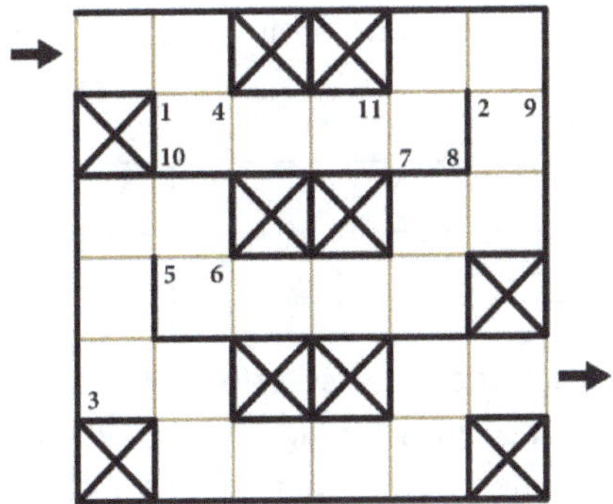

This exact Maze cipher was utilised during a Treasure Hunt for one of Cisco's teams. The hunt took place in person, navigating participants around the building until ultimately leading them back to their office.

Initially, the answer "CEFIOS" might seem like complete nonsense. However, the key lies in the small numbers embedded within the highlighted tiles. For instance, the letter C is accompanied by numbers 1, 4, and 10, indicating their respective positions in the sequence:

1	2	3	4	5	6	7	8	9	10	11
C			C						C	

Following this pattern, the remaining letters are filled in their designated positions.

1	2	3	4	5	6	7	8	9	10	11
C	I		C	O	O	F	F	I	C	

At this stage, some teams may already grasp the solution. However, for completionists, the final step involves determining where the last two letters fit within the remaining space, ultimately revealing the conclusive solution.

1	2	3	4	5	6	7	8	9	10	11
C	I	S	C	O	O	F	F	I	C	E

It's clear that the final solution, **"Cisco Office,"** could leave participants questioning exactly where to search. They might wonder: Which part of the office? That's why it's vital to provide clear, precise instructions. In this particular case, it was the first time the treasure hunt led participants to the office space, and the next clue was prominently displayed on the front door. However, thoroughly testing the final location is key to ensuring participants don't waste valuable time searching aimlessly. The clearer your instructions, the smoother the experience will be for everyone involved.

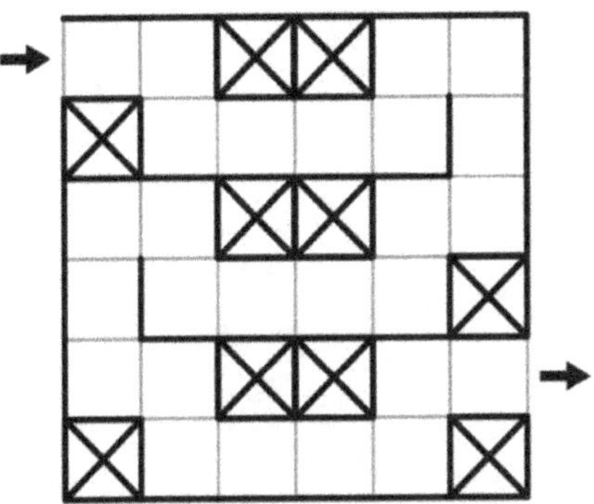

To create your own maze cipher, you can use this template and follow these simple steps:
1. Create the message you want to encrypt. Shorter messages, preferably below 15 characters, are recommended for clarity.
2. Identify the positions of the corresponding letters in the maze and highlight the corresponding tiles in the template. If you repeat letters, ensure to include indicators showing where each letter appears! Otherwise, participants may struggle to decipher the message.
3. Have someone test your final cipher to confirm that it's possible for participants to solve.

CHAPTER 3
FLAGS

CAN YOU TRY SOLVING THIS CIPHER ON YOUR OWN?

Flags of the world! Finally, something familiar. While some flags may be more recognisable than others, most people tend to immediately understand that they are dealing with countries and that this is the key to solving the cipher.

What was your first idea? Most people start by associating each flag with its respective country. In this case, you see the flags of Portugal, Canada, Thailand, Switzerland, Armenia, Germany, Greece, and Italy. If you take the first letter (or the last letter, which is another common method of encryption) of each country's name, you get:

- First letters: PCTSAGGI
- Last letters: LADDAYEY

Neither sequence makes any sense, even after rearranging letters. It appears the simplest solution wasn't the correct one (although in the majority of cases, it is, and you can definitely encrypt your cipher this way). But don't give up; we can dig deeper.

Now, look at the image behind the flags: a city skyline. This can be a significant hint. Let's consider the capital cities of these countries:

Portugal: Lisbon
Canada: Ottawa
Thailand: Bangkok
Switzerland: Bern
Armenia: Yerevan
Germany: Berlin
Greece: Athens
Italy: Rome

Let's try again using the first or last letter of each capital city's name. Starting with the first letters, we get **LOBBY BAR**. This was a very familiar place for the Cisco team, who had a nice café and bar in the lobby of their office building. They immediately knew where to go to search for the next step.

Replicating this cipher is quite easy; you just need to choose the level of difficulty.

The easiest method is to use only the countries. You can either use the first letter or the last letter (beware, using the last letter is much more difficult than it seems). For example, you can encrypt the word "HELLO" using the flags of:

- First letter of countries: Hungary, Ecuador, Latvia, Lebanon, Oman
- Last letter of countries: Bangladesh, France, Israel, Portugal, Morocco

The second layer of this clue involves encrypting the message using the names of the capital cities corresponding to the countries' flags.

The third and most complex method is to encrypt a message using the countries' currencies.

The overall difficulty levels of this cipher are as follows:

Method	Example for "Hello"	Difficulty
First Letter of the Country	Hungary, Ecuador, Latvia, Lebanon, Oman	★
First Letter of the Capital City	Vietnam (Hanoi), Scotland (Edinburgh), Peru (Lima), Great Britain (London), Norway (Oslo)	★★
Last Letter of the Country	Bangladesh, France, Israel, Portugal, Morocco	★★★★
First Letter of the Currency	Ukraine (Hryvnia), Finland (Euro), Turkey (Lira), Bulgaria (Lev), Mauritania (Ouguiya)	★★★★★★
Last Letter of the Capital City	Scotland (Edinburgh), North Macedonia (Skopje), South Korea (Seoul), Afghanistan (Kabul), Uruguay (Montevideo)	★★★★★★★

I wouldn't advise going beyond a 2-star difficulty level for your treasure hunts unless your audience is highly experienced. Tougher encryptions can easily cause teams to get stuck, leading to frustration rather than enjoyment. Often, simplifying the process is the best route, especially when participants are doing this just for fun. A well-balanced challenge that keeps things exciting without being overly complicated will always lead to a more satisfying experience.

You can find examples of countries, capital cities, and currencies in the table below, all sorted alphabetically. To create your own Flag cipher, start by picking a message to encrypt. Then, choose your preferred method. Remember, for longer messages, simpler methods work best.

	Countries	Capital Cities	Currency
A	Australia Argentina	Amsterdam Ankara	Afghani
B	Belgium Brazil	Bangkok Bratislava	Bolivar Boliviano
C	China Canada	Cairo Canberra	Colón Cedi
D	Denmark	Dublin Dakar	Dinar Dollar
E	Ecuador Egypt	Edinburgh	Euro
F	Finland France	Freetown Funafuti	Forint Franc
G	Germany Georgia	Georgetown Guatemala City	Guarani
H	Honduras Hungary	Havana Helsinki	Hryvnia
I	India Iceland	Islamabad	None

J	Jamaica Japan	Jakarta	None
K	Kazakhstan Kenya	Kingston Kyiv	Koruna Krona
L	Latvia Lebanon	Lisbon Ljubljana	Lira Lev
M	Mexico Malaysia	Madrid Manila	Manat
N	New Zealand Norway	Nairobi New Delhi	Naira
O	Oman	Oslo Ottawa	Ouguiya
P	Portugal Panama	Paris Prague	Peso Pound Sterling
Q	Qatar	Quito	Quetzal
R	Romania Russia	Riga Rome	Real Rupee
S	Spain Sweden	Santiago Seoul	Shekel Sol
T	Thailand Turkey	Teheran Tokyo	Taka Tenge
U	United Kingdom United States	Ulaanbaatar	None
V	Vietnam Venezuela	Vienna Vilnius	Vatu
W	None	Warsaw Wellington	Won
X	None	None	None
Y	Yemen	Yerevan	Yen
Z	Zambia Zimbabwe	Zagreb	Zloty

CHAPTER 4
CAESAR CIPHER

OFYU DMVF JT
PVUTJEF BU UIF
QMBZHSPVOE

CAN YOU TRY SOLVING THIS CIPHER ON YOUR OWN?

As you might guess from the name, the famous Caesar cipher is named after Julius Caesar, the Roman emperor. Caesar reportedly used this cipher in his private correspondence to keep his messages safe from prying eyes. It's a simple substitution cipher where each letter in the text is shifted a certain number of places up or down the alphabet.

What was your first thought when you saw this particular cipher? The nonsense text immediately signals that something's off. You can't read the message backwards, nor can you shuffle the letters in each word to make sense of it (by the way, shuffling letters is another fun and easy cipher if you want to explore that).

So, when you look at this jumbled text, your only option is to figure out what each letter stands for. If you tried the simplest shift and replaced each letter with the next one in the alphabet—changing "A" to "B," "B" to "C," and so on—then congratulations! You just solved the Caesar cipher.

Encrypted	O	F	Y	U	D	M	V	F	J	T	P	V	U	T	J	E	F
Original	N	E	X	T	C	L	U	E	I	S	O	U	T	S	I	D	E

Encrypted	B	U	U	I	F	Q	M	B	Z	H	S	P	V	O	E
Original	A	T	T	H	E	P	L	A	Y	G	R	O	U	N	D

With the answer "**next clue is outside at the playground**," you've got a clear direction. Now, you know exactly where to go and search for the next step.

Julius Caesar himself used a shift of three to protect his messages. For example, "A" would be encrypted to "D," "B" to "E," and so on. There are up to 25 possible shifts (excluding the identity shift where the alphabet remains unchanged), but for your treasure hunt, I recommend keeping the shift to 1. This makes it a simple cipher that almost everyone should be able to decode. If you plan to include hints, you can increase the shift count to add a bit more challenge.

Even though the Caesar cipher might seem a bit basic for more experienced players, I genuinely recommend using it—or another straightforward cipher—especially in the early stages of your treasure hunt. Starting off with a simple cipher is fantastic because it allows your participants to solve clues quickly and build their confidence. Think about it: when participants encounter a clue they can crack in just a minute or two, it's a real boost to their excitement and morale. Imagine being in their shoes—if you had to ask for help at every step, it might feel frustrating or discouraging. It could even make you wonder if the game is meant for you.

By using easy riddles like the Caesar cipher, you're giving everyone a chance to shine and feel capable. It shows that the game is designed for them to enjoy and succeed. So, keeping clues manageable and encouraging will make the whole experience more fun and rewarding for everyone involved. The goal is to make each participant feel like they're making progress and having a great time.

To replicate the Caesar cipher, just follow these easy steps:

Choose Your Message: Start by picking the message you want to encrypt. The Caesar cipher works well for both short and long texts, but don't get carried away and try encrypting an entire book! Keep it manageable and fun.

Pick a Shift Number: Next, decide on your shift number. A simple shift of 1 is a great starting point and keeps things straightforward. If you're feeling a bit adventurous and want to use a more complex shift, consider giving a hint about the shift somewhere in your clue or description. This way, participants won't have to guess through countless shifts to decode your message.

Original	A	B	C	D	E	F	G	H	I	J	K	L	M
Shifted 1	B	C	D	E	F	G	H	I	J	K	L	M	N
Shifted 2	C	D	E	F	G	H	I	J	K	L	M	N	O
Shifted 3	D	E	F	G	H	I	J	K	L	M	N	O	P

Original	N	O	P	Q	R	S	T	U	V	W	X	Y	Z
Shifted 1	O	P	Q	R	S	T	U	V	W	X	Y	Z	A
Shifted 2	P	Q	R	S	T	U	V	W	X	Y	Z	A	B
Shifted 3	Q	R	S	T	U	V	W	X	Y	Z	A	B	C

These tables show how each letter of the alphabet changes with shifts of 1, 2, and 3 positions. For instance, with a shift of 1, "A" becomes "B;" with a shift of 2, "A" becomes "C," and with a shift of 3, "A" becomes "D."

CHAPTER 5
PICTOGRAMS

CAN YOU TRY SOLVING THIS CIPHER ON YOUR OWN?

Now, let's dive into a purely visual clue. No text, just some pictures or pictograms. Your task is to make sense of these images and figure out the solution. It's a bit of a brain teaser, but it's also a lot of fun!

For those of you who have been to London and used its public transportation system, the first pictogram might look familiar. It may even be familiar to those who have never been to the UK; that's how famous this brand is. It resembles the logo of Transport for London (TfL). TfL encompasses various modes of transport, but what stands out about London? Buses and the Underground! If we wanted the first part of the clue to be bus-related, we could have used a different pictogram. So, maybe this clue is hinting at the London Underground system.

Now, let's talk about the other two pictograms. One shows a golf scene, and the other a crown. This is where your creativity comes into play. It's easier said than done, but that's what makes a treasure hunt exciting. You'll often find that some teams crack the clue in seconds, while others may need more time—or even a hint. It's usually a 50/50 split. How about you? Did it click right away, or did it take some extra thought?

Let's break it down: the crown symbolizes a king. The golf pictogram is a bit more complex. Notice the flag with "4/4?" What do you call it when you complete a hole in the exact number of strokes predetermined? That's right—a par.

Now, putting it all together: we have "Underground," "par," and "king." Mix those last two, and you get "parking." So, the next clue leads you to the **underground parking** area.

When you send people to an underground parking garage (or any large, complex location), one of the biggest risks is that participants might end up searching everywhere, unsure of where to find the next step. Parking garages, in particular, are vast and can be confusing, and it's not exactly safe to run around in them. To reduce this risk, make sure to place the next clue in a very visible spot, such as right at the entrance. This way, participants can easily and safely find the clue without having to explore the entire area.

Making the clue location easy to find doesn't detract from the fun—in fact, it keeps the game moving smoothly and ensures everyone stays safe. Plus, it adds to the excitement when participants quickly locate the next step and can move on to the next challenge.

Replicating the Pictogram cipher is all about creativity and thinking outside of the box. Instead of using a crown to symbolise a king, you could have opted for a chess king pictogram to be more precise or even an image of a king. Instead of the golf pictogram, you could have used a car park sign or something entirely different to convey the same message. There are countless ways to recreate this cipher and you have endless possibilities to choose images that make the riddle challenging yet solvable.

To help with the ideation phase, here are some other examples of pictogram ciphers. Can you guess the solution based on these pictures? You can check the next page for the correct answer.

Top left: Microwave
Top right: New York meeting room (this works great if you have office areas named after cities or countries)
Bottom left: Second Floor (ensure the clue is easy to spot as soon as people arrive)
Bottom right: KFC - Kentucky Fried Chicken

Creating a cipher using only pictures or pictograms requires some creativity. This method works especially well for short messages that direct participants to a specific location.

One great way to find the perfect pictograms is to use image search, but my favourite website for this is thenounproject.com. It has millions of pictograms available for any word you can think of. Just type in the word you want a pictogram for, and you can create your clue in no time.

CHAPTER 6
PHONETIC ALPHABET

LIMA: 7

KILO: 15

INDIA: 2

TANGO: 5

ROMEO: 3,10,12,16

FOXTROT: 1,6

BRAVO: 11

SIERRA: 4

MIKE: 19

ECHO: 13

ALPHA: 14

OSCAR: 8,9,17,18

CAN YOU TRY SOLVING THIS CIPHER ON YOUR OWN?

Have you ever heard of the phonetic alphabet? It's one of those things that most people know exists, but unless you work in certain industries, you might not be very familiar with it. Its history is actually pretty fascinating and goes all the way back to the early 20th century.

Imagine a time when radios crackled with static and telephones hummed with interference. Misunderstandings were common, especially when trying to spell out important information. The need for a better system was clear and thus began the journey of creating the phonetic alphabet. After World War II, it became even more obvious that we needed a universal system. So, brilliant minds from around the world got together and developed what we now know as the NATO phonetic alphabet.

This new alphabet, adopted by the International Civil Aviation Organization (ICAO) in 1956 and later by NATO, wasn't just a random collection of words. Each word was carefully chosen for its distinctiveness and clarity. For example, "Alpha," "Bravo," and "Charlie" sound very different from each other, even over a poor connection. This way, if a pilot radioed "Charlie" instead of "Delta," there'd be no confusion.

So, you can see where we're going with this. Each of these words represents a letter of the alphabet—Alpha stands for A, Bravo for B, Charlie for C, and so on.

Next to the words, you'll notice numbers. These numbers show two things: how many times this letter is used in the answer and where it stands in the order. To decipher this riddle, you start with Foxtrot because it has the number 1. Then, you continue with India (number 2), followed by Romeo, and so on, until you reveal the answer: **First Floor Breakroom**. This leads you to a very specific location to search for the next clue.

To replicate this cipher, start by choosing a message

(short ones work best). Use the table below to see which letter corresponds to its phonetic equivalent. Remember to add numbers next to each word so the participants can identify the order of the letters in the message.

Letter	Phonetic Word	Letter	Phonetic Word
A	Alpha	N	November
B	Bravo	O	Oscar
C	Charlie	P	Papa
D	Delta	Q	Quebec
E	Echo	R	Romeo
F	Foxtrot	S	Sierra
G	Golf	T	Tango
H	Hotel	U	Uniform
I	India	V	Victor
J	Juliett	W	Whiskey
K	Kilo	X	Xray
L	Lima	Y	Yankee
M	Mike	Z	Zulu

Combining Ciphers and Creating Multi-Layered Ciphers

Multi-layered ciphers add an extra level of complexity to your puzzles by incorporating multiple steps. In these ciphers, you won't get the final answer right away. Instead, each layer reveals part of the solution, which helps you decode the next layer, and so on, until you reach the final answer.

While multi-layered ciphers are intriguing and challenging, they also make the puzzle significantly more complex. This added difficulty can be great for advanced puzzle competitions or for people who want to be challenged and dedicate time to find the solution, but it is overwhelming for a simple treasure hunt.

If you're curious about how to combine different types of ciphers, here's a gentle introduction. Consider using pictograms alongside the phonetic alphabet. Instead of using the phonetic words directly, you could represent each word with a pictogram. Participants would first need to decode the pictograms and then use the phonetic alphabet to decipher the final message.

This method can add an interesting twist, but it's important to ensure that it doesn't make the puzzle too difficult for your audience. Balancing complexity with clarity helps keep the experience enjoyable for everyone. You'll find more examples of easy, multi-layered ciphers in the following chapters.

CHAPTER 7
HIEROGLYPHICS

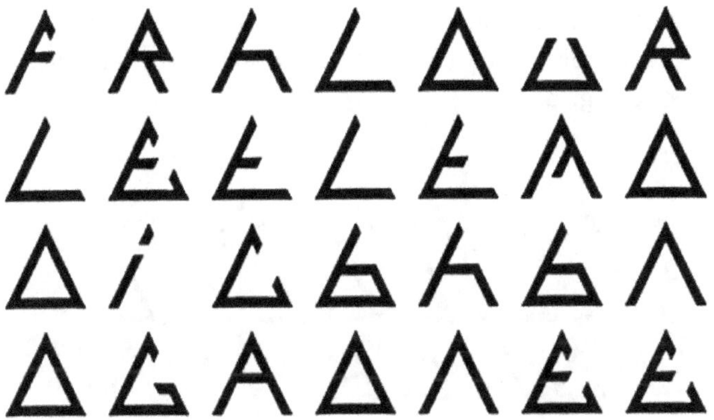

CAN YOU TRY SOLVING THIS CIPHER ON YOUR OWN?

When you first glanced at these hieroglyphics or symbols, what ran through your mind? Did they remind you of letters? Did you even try to read them? If so, you're already on the right path. Think of this as a secret alphabet, one that's a bit tricky to recognise at first. It's actually the English alphabet, just disguised in a clever way. Once you start spotting the letters, it all begins to make sense. Every letter from A to Z is hidden in this alphabet. Firstly, you need to identify which letters are creating the message, and the next challenge is figuring out how to read them.

Here's a little tip: start reading from the top left corner, move down the first column to the bottom, then jump back up to the top of the second column, and repeat. Continue this way, column by column, until you've worked through the entire grid.

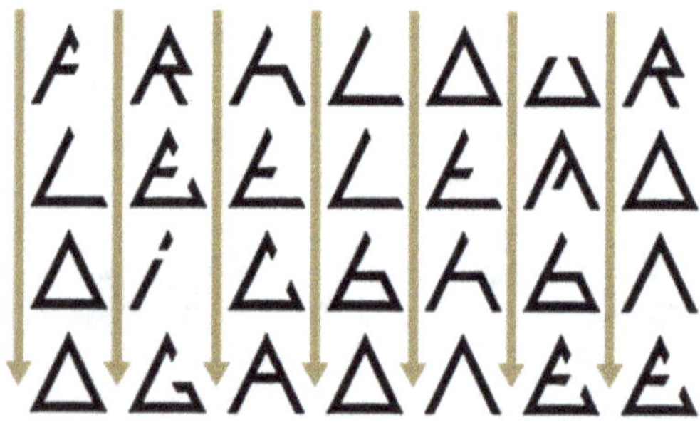

Once you've cracked the code, you'll uncover a message guiding you to the next clue: it's at the **8th floor in call booth number 1**. See how clearly the location is revealed once you decipher the text. At first, these kinds of ciphers can seem tricky, but the solution is hidden in plain sight. This method of encoding, where the alphabet is written in a hidden way, is ideal for longer messages.

This is also a perfect example of a multilayer cipher.

Unlike simple text block ciphers, it's best to stick to straightforward patterns here. Start by figuring out which symbol matches each letter, and then focus on understanding the reading pattern. Keeping it simple will help ensure your teams don't get stuck too often or need too many hints. But if you're looking for an extra challenge, text block ciphers can be more complex, but only involve a single layer.

To create your own cipher, start by deciding on the message you want to encode. This cipher works especially well with longer messages, so feel free to get creative. Once you've got your message in mind, use the alphabet example below. Finally, you'll need to select a pattern to encrypt your message. Just keep in mind that simple patterns tend to work best since multi-layer ciphers are already pretty challenging on their own.

CHAPTER 8
STORY CIPHER

congratulatIons, treasure seeker bold!
you've cracked the code, let the story uNfold.
but beware, The road ahead is sly,
wHere only the sharpest minds apply.

your next clue hidEs in shadows deep,
where seCrets lie, and riddles sleep.
every puzzle hAs its key,
and every mystery begs to be Free.

trust your instincts, keep Eyes keen,
for The treasure's nearer than it may seem.
ready to continuE, to seek and find?
let the hunt unRavel, one step behind!

step by step, you'll fInd your prize,
As the treasure awaits before your eyes!

CAN YOU TRY SOLVING THIS CIPHER ON YOUR OWN?

This looks rather like a simple poem at first glance, but does it contain a hidden message? Look closer. Have you noticed the strange capital letters nestled in the middle of some words? If you have, then you're already on the right track to solving the clue! Each verse contains one word with a capital letter hidden inside it. By finding all these capitalised letters, you'll uncover the answer: **in the cafeteria**.

congratulatIons, treasure seeker bold!
you've cracked the code, let the story uNfold.
but beware, The road ahead is sly,
wHere only the sharpest minds apply.

your next clue hidEs in shadows deep,
where seCrets lie, and riddles sleep.
every puzzle hAs its key,
and every mystery begs to be Free.

trust your instincts, keep Eyes keen,
for The treasure's nearer than it may seem.
ready to continuE, to seek and find?
let the hunt unRavel, one step behind!

step by step, you'll fInd your prize,
As the treasure awaits before your eyes!

This cipher technique works brilliantly for both short and long messages. You can weave it into a fictional story, a poem, or even slip it into real instructions or educational material. However, use it with care—unless you're aiming for a particularly playful approach, this may not be the ideal method for getting your employees to absorb the content of your Code of Conduct or Terms of Service!

If you're seeking a creative spark to craft your story, why not try AI tools? They can generate a compelling narrative or poem in just seconds, helping you add that extra flair to your ciphered content.

There are multiple variations of this cipher. This is the simplest, where a single capital letter is placed in a random word in each verse. These capital letters stand out, making it easy to spot them and piece together the hidden message. Most participants should be able to solve this type of cipher without any issues. Alternatively, you can remove a single letter from every row—these spelling mistakes are usually obvious and common enough to catch attention.

If you're aiming for a more challenging setup, try placing a capital letter at the start of each sentence to spell out the clue. Since sentences naturally begin with capital letters, this method blends seamlessly into the text, making it nearly invisible to the casual observer. For an extra twist, you could format sentences so that the new sentence continues on the same line rather than starting on a new row, which adds an additional layer of difficulty. This approach might stump some groups, but those who crack the code will likely appreciate the cleverness of the cipher.

Alternatively, you can place a capital letter at the end of each sentence or use bold or underlined text instead of capital letters. The key is to make the letters that form the cipher stand out just enough for participants to spot and piece together the hidden message. Here are some additional examples of story cipher hiding the word "treasure" using different encryption methods:

1. First Letter of Each Row. Difficulty: ★

Twists and turns through paths unknown,
Riddles lead where winds have blown.
Eager hearts, a quest to find,
A hidden trove, by clues designed.
Seek the signs both far and near,
Unveil secrets buried here.
Reach the goal, the prize in sight,
End the hunt with joy and light.

2. Spelling Errors. Difficulty: ★

Get ready to sart. Don't ovecomplicate things and prpare to go with the flow of the gme. Think outide the box, and trst your instincts. You've navigated challenges befoe, and this will be no diffrent. You've got this!

3. First Letter of Each Sentence. Difficulty: ★★

Today's the day for the epic office treasure hunt! Racing around like kids, everyone's pumped. Each team gets some wacky clues. As the timer starts, chaos and laughter ensue. Sneaking through cubicles, you all are seeking the right locations. Under desks and behind plants, search everywhere. Reaching the final spot, you'll find a stash of pizza and drinks. Everyone, now it's time to find the solution and get closer to victory.

4. Last Letter of Each Row. Difficulty: ★★★

in our office, where we start,
you'll become an explorer
and follow the path where lights shine
to find the hidden area,
search the office corridors,
and even ask the game guru,
a mystery to discover,
you find the answer if you endure.

When organising your first treasure hunt, I'd suggest starting with a simpler difficulty level. For a successful game, it's essential that 50-70% of the clues are relatively easy to solve. By keeping some steps straightforward, you allow participants to build momentum and gain confidence as they progress. The goal is to make the experience fun and engaging, not frustrating. When people feel like they're making steady progress, they're more likely to enjoy the journey and feel satisfied with their progress. After all, the office treasure hunt should be a fun team-building challenge, not a test of patience and problem-solving skills.

While this advice might seem obvious, the game is often much trickier for the participants than you'd expect. As the organiser, it's easy to assume the clues are straightforward, but they're often tougher for players to solve than they seem to you.

CHAPTER 9
PICTURE

CAN YOU TRY SOLVING THIS CIPHER ON YOUR OWN?

This is the first and only cipher in the treasure hunt, where I wasn't entirely sure you'd be able to solve it. The success of this puzzle can depend on the resolution of the screen you're using, as well as the print quality. So if you managed to solve it, that's fantastic! As you can see, using a cipher like this can be tricky, which is why I recommend printing it out to avoid issues caused by different screen brightness or colour settings.

To solve this cipher, you need to carefully examine the picture. This type of puzzle is perfect for kicking off a treasure hunt. Start by printing the image and handing a copy to each team at the first location. The challenge lies in closely observing the picture to find the hidden message. If you look carefully, you'll notice letters scattered around the image. Gather those letters, piece them together, and you'll reveal the solution—"**Lobby**" in this case.

Picture ciphers like this one are especially fun for themed treasure hunts. Whether it's Halloween, Thanksgiving, Christmas, or any other occasion, you can tailor the image to fit the theme. The key is to blend the letters into the picture—make them visible but not too obvious. It's all about finding that sweet spot where the letters stand out enough to be discovered when you look closely but not at first glance.

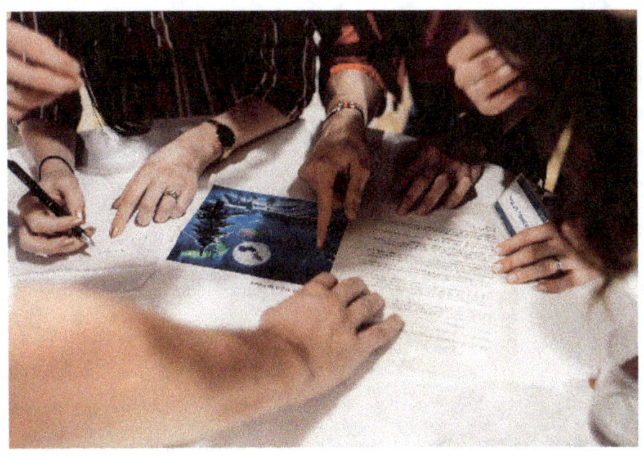

This type of clue works best for short messages, ideally a single word. In these cases, it's easy to shuffle a few letters to form the solution. However, it becomes much more challenging with longer messages.

If you want to use a longer message with a picture cipher, consider colour-coding—assign each word a colour and use those colours for the corresponding letters hidden in the picture.

For an even more challenging twist, you could include all the letters in the picture **except** those that form the solution. This approach takes longer to solve because participants will first need to identify all the letters in the picture, then figure out which ones are missing, and finally piece together the solution. If you decide to try this method, try using a heterogram—a word, phrase, or sentence where no letter appears more than once—so could KITCHEN / SHOWER / LOCKERS be a good location for your treasure hunt? I'll leave this to you.

CHAPTER 10
PIGPEN CIPHER

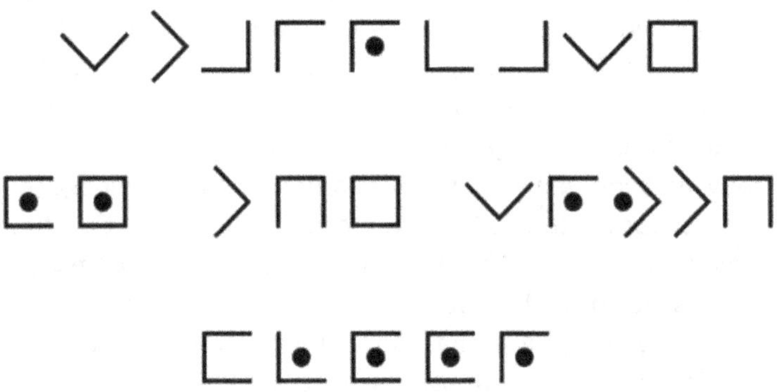

Hint:

CAN YOU TRY SOLVING THIS CIPHER ON YOUR OWN?

Imagine a secret message hidden in plain sight—so well disguised that only those familiar with the code can decipher it without any hints. That's exactly what the Pigpen cipher, also known as the Freemason cipher or Masonic alphabet, is all about. If you're already in the know, you might crack the code effortlessly. But if you're new to this intriguing cipher, even the hint might leave you puzzled at first.

Let me take you on a little adventure into the world of the Pigpen cipher. This was actually the secret code of choice for Freemasons, a fascinating group with a rich history full of mysterious rituals and symbols. They used it to keep their messages hidden from prying eyes, much like they've kept many of their traditions and knowledge in secrecy for centuries. Now, you can do the same! It's a fun way to turn your message into a mysterious, seemingly impossible-to-read scribble.

Picture this: a grid that looks like a game of tic-tac-toe, but instead of Xs and Os, it's filled with unique symbols representing the letters of the alphabet. To create or crack the code, you simply match each letter with its corresponding symbol. It's like having the secret language hidden within a grid of lines and dots—adding a bit of mystery to even the simplest of messages.

Here's how you start: the hint uses 26 open spaces, perfect for the 26 letters of the English alphabet. The first step is to fill in each letter of the alphabet, beginning from the top left. By doing this, you'll create the following Freemason alphabet:

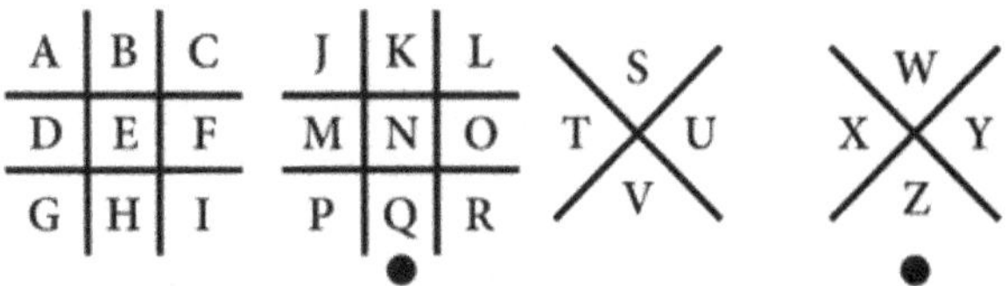

When you piece together the symbols with corresponding letters, you get the answer **"staircase on the sixth floor"**—another location in our treasure hunt.

The Pigpen cipher is a fantastic tool, whether you're encoding short or longer messages. The Masonic alphabet has a unique charm, and it feels like a waste only to use it for single-word solutions. Instead, try creating at least a short sentence with it. This way, you'll get to use more of its letters and really make the cipher come alive.

To use the Pigpen cipher, start by deciding on the message you want to encrypt. Once you have it, simply rewrite, or take screenshots of the letters you need and piece them together. I recommend adding a hint with this cipher, as it can be tricky, especially for those unfamiliar with it. A small nudge in the right direction can make all the difference. The hint could be the same one provided earlier in the chapter, or you might want to make it even easier by filling in a letter or two. This gentle clue helps participants stay on track by guiding them to complete the remaining letters without giving too much away.

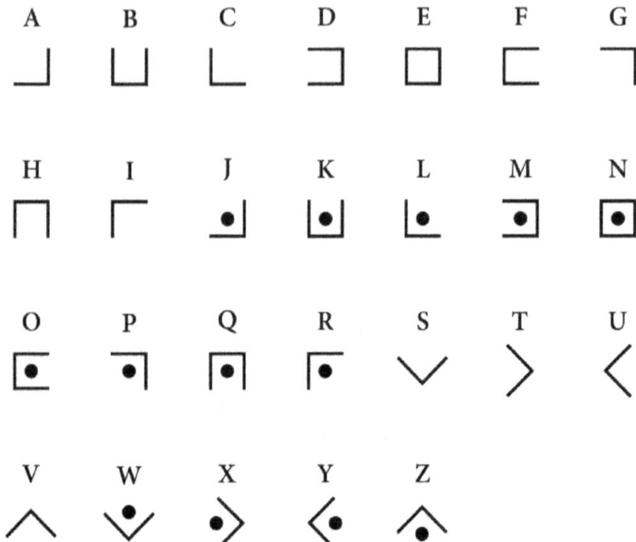

Example of a hint:

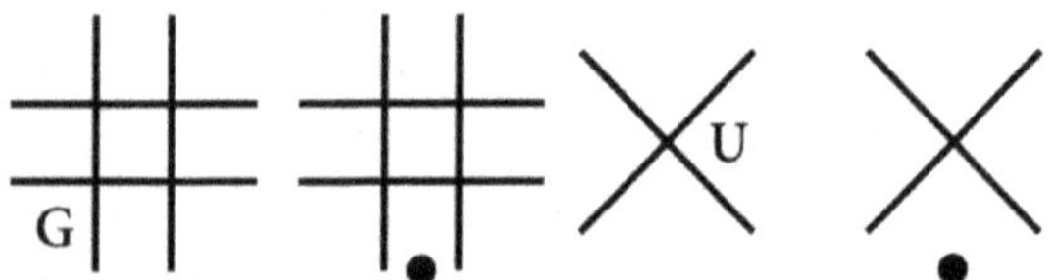

CHAPTER 11
ALCHEMY (CHEMISTRY CIPHER)

$$O_4F_2N_1$$

$$S_4C_2O_3$$

CAN YOU TRY SOLVING THIS CIPHER ON YOUR OWN?

Oh no, it's been ages since high school, and chemistry was never my strong suit! Can you relate? If the thought of elements and molecules makes you nervous, don't worry—I've been there too. But here's the good news: this cipher isn't really about testing your chemistry knowledge. It might look like it came straight out of a science textbook, but trust me, it's actually about something entirely different.

The goal of every treasure hunt is to create challenges that are fun and engaging, but not too tough once you dive in. So, going with a full-on scientific approach might not be the best for everyone. But it allows for a perfect disguise and just like any magic trick, that's what it's all about. So, let's break down this Alchemy cipher together. First, we've got the elements, and then we have the number of atoms of each element.

Now, in real life, most molecules and chemical compounds are made up of just a few key elements: carbon (C), hydrogen (H), oxygen (O), and nitrogen (N). These four are like the building blocks of life—they combine in all sorts of ways to create everything from the air we breathe to the food we eat.

But here's the thing: while this cipher looks like a complicated chemical formula, it's actually a lot simpler than it seems. So, let's strip away the chemistry disguise and focus on the letters and numbers next to each one. Maybe that's a hint?

Remember a few chapters ago when we talked about the Caesar cipher, where you had to shift letters by a certain amount? This cipher works in a similar way, but with a twist: each letter has its own shift, determined by the number of atoms next to the element. Pretty clever, right? It looks like a real chemical molecule, but in reality, it's just a message in disguise.

The message starts with 4 atoms of Oxygen (O4). If we shift the letter "O" by 4, we'll get "S." The second letter is "F" and has a number 2. If we shift "F" by 2 letters, we get "H." You continue this way with all the letters in the cipher. And when you crack it, the answer—"**SHOWER**"—will lead you to the next treasure hunt location.

This alchemy cipher works best with short messages. To create one yourself, start with the location and use the most common elements:

Carbon (C) is the backbone of most molecules and shows up in everything from food to fuel.
Hydrogen (H) is the most abundant element in the universe and is crucial in water and organic compounds.
Oxygen (O) is essential for life and is found in water and the air we breathe.
Nitrogen (N) makes up a big part of the air and is key in building proteins in our bodies.

These elements are like nature's LEGO bricks—they combine to create all sorts of things. So take them and mix these "bricks" with other elements from the periodic table to fit your cipher perfectly. Now, in the real world, you can't just mix any elements together—nature has its rules. But for this cipher, it works like a charm. Just don't forget to add the atomic number because that's the key to the shift—how many letters the participant needs to move to reveal the answer.

CHAPTER 12
ANCIENT MANUSCRIPT

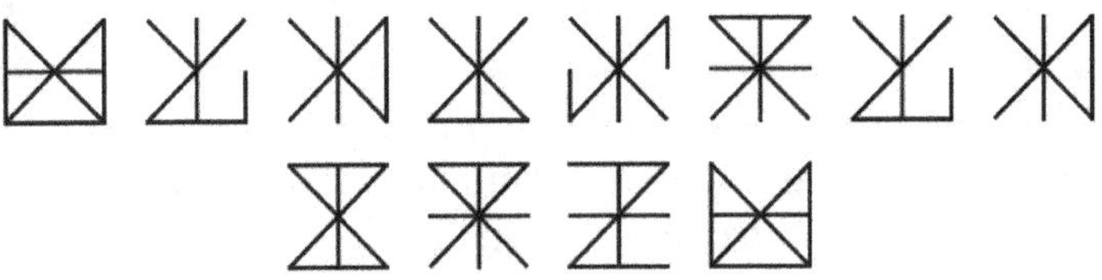

Hint:

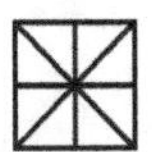

CAN YOU TRY SOLVING THIS CIPHER ON YOUR OWN?

What are you looking at? Does it remind you of a runic alphabet straight out of a fantasy world, or maybe it looks like an East Asian script, perhaps something like Mandarin? At first glance, this scramble can be pretty confusing because it's completely unfamiliar. So, what exactly is it, and how do you make sense of it?

Did the hint help you to figure it out right away, or did it take some time? When people see the hint, they might notice that none of the shapes in the cipher seems to match it. Is that intentional, or just a coincidence? And what does it all mean? As usual, the hint is there to guide you. Even if it's not immediately clear, it's meant to steer you in the right direction. In this case, the hint is a box filled with lines going in all directions, with no empty spaces. So, what happens if you make each symbol in the cipher look like the one in the hint?

Here's the trick: each symbol in the cipher is missing some lines that are present in the hint's shape. If you start to slowly fill in those missing lines, something magical happens—letters of the Latin alphabet begin to appear. Soon enough, you've deciphered the clue, which reveals the phrase **"treasure hunt."**

This cipher seems complex at first but becomes simple once you focus on the hint and fill in the blanks. The letters form words and sentences that guide participants to the next location in a treasure hunt. It's a beautiful and creative visual cipher. It works well even for longer messages because once you understand how to solve it, it only takes a few seconds to decipher the whole message. This will work really well if you want to give very specific directions to the next location of the treasure hunt.

If you want to encrypt your own message using this cipher, it's really simple. Just match the symbols to each letter and piece your message together. That's all there is to it! Once your message is ready, think about the hint you'd like to provide for your participants. You could choose a visual hint, like the one I shared earlier in this chapter, or go for a verbal clue, such as "Fill in the blanks."

Even with a hint, not everyone may crack the cipher right away—and that's perfectly fine! Some participants might need a little extra help. In those cases, you can always offer an additional hint, gently steering them in the right direction when needed.

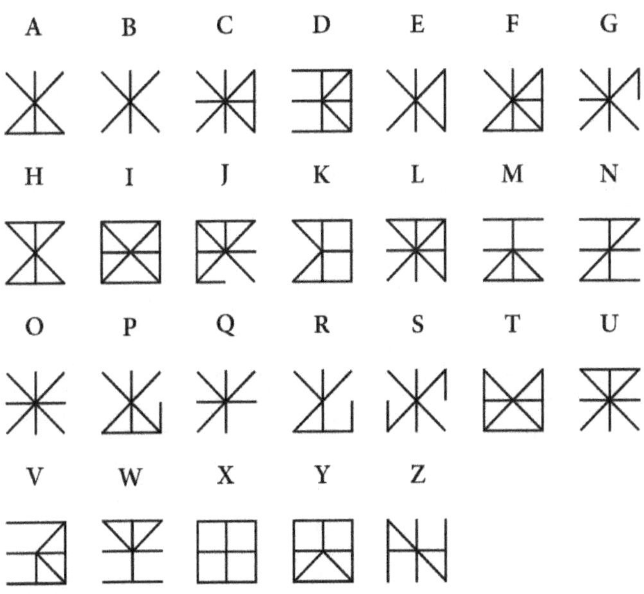

CHAPTER 13
PHONEBOOK CIPHER

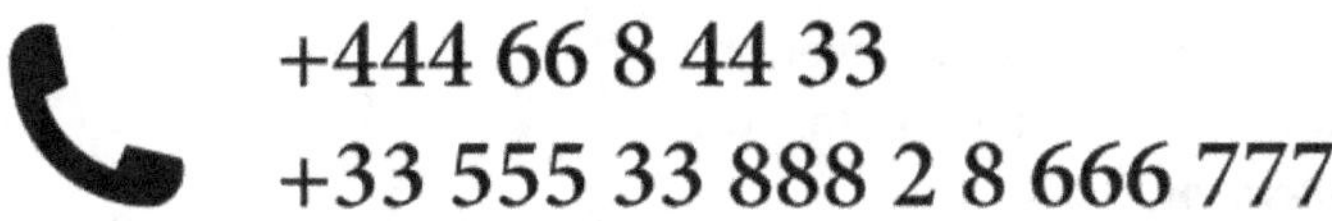

CAN YOU TRY SOLVING THIS CIPHER ON YOUR OWN?

At first glance, it might look like you've stumbled upon a really odd phone number—maybe too long or just strange. You might even wonder, "Is that even a real phone number?". Of course, it isn't. That's where the phone book cipher comes into play.

This cipher is all about translating letters into numbers using a phone keypad. Remember when we used to send text messages by pressing numbers that would turn into letters? That's the secret behind this cipher. So, if you open up your phone's keypad and start typing in those numbers, you'll uncover the hidden message: **"In the elevator."**

Two decades ago, we did this without thinking, typing out numbers on our keypads to form our texts. Even though technology has moved on, muscle memory still lingers. And from my experience, that's why most people (sorry, Gen Alpha) are able to figure out this cipher without much hassle.

There are two ways to use the phone book cipher, so pick the one you like best:

1. Encrypt a Message as Some Odd Phone Number.

One way to use the phone book cipher is to encode a message as a series of phone numbers. This method is perfect for short messages—just a few "phone numbers," one for each long word, and your message is cleverly hidden. If the words are too short (like pronouns, prepositions or conjunctions), then you can combine them together in a single phone number to make the cipher more consistent and believable.

2. Encrypt a Message as a Broken Text.

Another approach is to make the cipher look like a broken text message filled with numbers that actually spell out the final message.

This technique is particularly fun because it lets you encode even longer messages. For example, in the picture, the numbers decode to **"The next clue is in the elevator."** You can easily extend this in your version of the game to include more detailed instructions.

The key to making this work is to design the cipher so that it looks just like a real text message—this creates a perfect, built-in hint that subtly nudges participants toward the solution. One of the best ways to do this is by sending the message as an actual text and then taking a screenshot. This not only makes it look authentic but also serves as a bulletproof hint, ensuring participants know exactly where to focus their attention. Plus, the familiarity of a text message format makes the process more intuitive and fun, adding an extra layer of satisfaction when they finally decode the message.

CHAPTER 14
EMOJI CIPHER

Hint: Do you know your music bands?

CAN YOU TRY SOLVING THIS CIPHER ON YOUR OWN?

The Emoji Cipher is always a crowd-pleaser—who doesn't love emojis? They're universal, expressing emotions, objects, and ideas in ways that go beyond language and culture. That's exactly why they work so well for encrypting a message in a treasure hunt. Since we use emojis every day, why not turn them into a fun challenge?

Let's dive into how it works using music artists represented by emojis. Once you've cracked which bands are hidden in the emojis, it's time to solve the cipher. Each emoji represents a word, and the numbers next to it are the key to finding specific letters within those words.

Here's how it works: First, figure out the word each emoji represents. For example, the first band is Arctic Monkeys. Once you know that, the emoji represents "monkey." If the number next to it is 4, you'll take the fourth letter of the word "monkey," which is K—that's your first letter. In the next row, you recognize the Spice Girls. Take the emoji for "spice" and look at the number—it's 3, so the third letter is I. Continue this process, and eventually, you'll uncover the answer: "**Kitchen Area.**"

The beauty of the Emoji Cipher is that you don't need to solve every single part to find the next clue. Once you've got most of the letters, you can usually fill in the blanks. So, even if one or two emojis stump you, you can still move forward.

This cipher is also fantastic for teamwork. Participants can split up responsibilities—some can focus on deciphering the bands, while others work on extracting the letters. It's a great way to get everyone involved and collaborating.

Emoji	Fraction	Letter		Emoji sequence	Band
🐒	4/6	K		❄️🐒🐒	Arctic Monkeys
🌶	3/5	I		🌶👧👧👧	Spice Girls
🔥	3/3	T		🔴🔥🌶🌶	Red Hot Chili Peppers
🥶	1/4	C		🥶▶️	Coldplay
🔨	5/8	H		🔨🎃🎃	Smashing Pumpkins
🟢	3/5	E		🟢📅	Green Day
🐉	6/6	N		🤔💬🐉🐉	Imagine Dragons
🦍	7/7	A		🦍🦍🦍	Gorillaz
🌹	1/4	R		🔫🔫🌹🌹	Guns N' Roses
🦅	1/5	E		🦅🦅	The Eagles
🫛	3/3	A		⚫👁🫛🫛	Black Eyed Peas

While this example uses music bands, you can adapt the theme to anything—famous movies, TV series, or even books and literature. The possibilities are endless with the Emoji Cipher and you can find countless of examples online.

When I used this for team-building at Slido, they had special emojis on Slack that represented different people in the company. I created a cipher using those emojis, and new hires had to figure out who those people were. It was a fun, engaging way for them to get to know their colleagues better using their own internal resources. As mentioned, there are countless ways how you can use this cipher and it's up to your creativity.

But to help you get started, here is a list of 30 famous music bands and artists that you can use to create your own emoji cipher.

 Arctic Monkeys
Spice Girls
Red Hot Chili Peppers
Coldplay
Smashing Pumpkins
Green Day
Imagine Dragons
Gorillaz
Guns N' Roses
The Eagles
Black Eyed Peas
Snoop Dogg
Oasis
Kiss
The Rolling Stones

 Beach Boys
The Police
Scorpions
Deadmau5
Fallout Boy
Panic! at the Disco
Deep Purple
Backstreet Boys
Atomic Kitten
Def Leppard
Queen
Heart
Radiohead
Alien Ant Farm
The Doors

CHAPTER 15
NINE MAN'S MORRIS

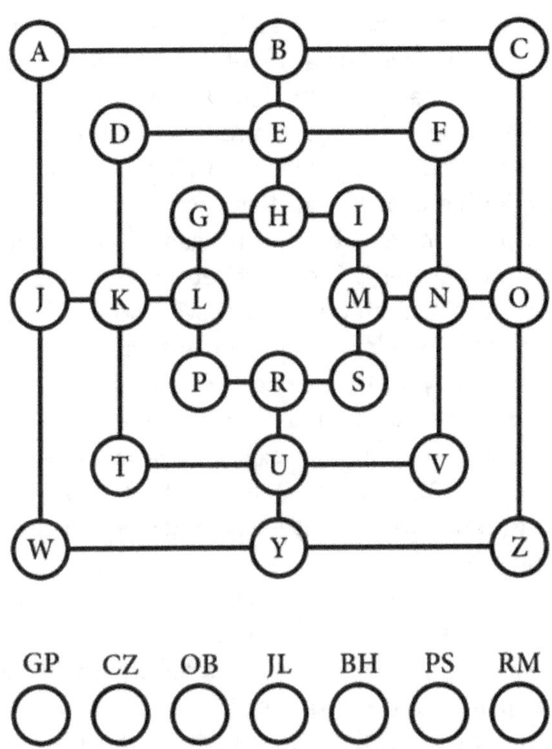

CAN YOU TRY SOLVING THIS CIPHER ON YOUR OWN?

Nine Men's Morris is a game that has truly stood the test of time—it's over 3,000 years old. This ancient game was so beloved that archaeologists have discovered boards carved into stone slabs and even on the walls of ancient temples. It was especially popular in the Roman Empire, where you can still find Morris boards etched into the stones of Roman ruins scattered across Europe. Imagine that—a game we can still play today, etched into history itself.

The game is played on a grid of three concentric squares connected by lines at the midpoints. The goal? Simple: to form a line of three pieces in a row. And believe it or not, that's also the goal of the Nine Men's Morris Cipher.

Now, let me explain how this ancient game transforms into a cipher. Instead of a blank game board, the Nine Men's Morris Cipher is filled with letters. However, there's a twist: the board only has 24 spaces, while the English alphabet has 26 letters. So, two letters are missing. If you're creating your own cipher, you might wonder which letters to leave out. Interestingly, some letters are rarely used in English—X and J, for example, appear in just 0.15% of words, Q in 0.095%, and Z in only 0.07%. So, you could choose to omit two of these rare letters when setting up your cipher board.

Just like in the game, the goal of our cipher is to make three in a row. But here's the catch: instead of seeing complete rows, you only see pairs of letters. For instance, if the first pair you see is G and P, your task is to find the letter that would sit between them on the game board. Letter L completes the trio and becomes the first letter in our ciphered message. As you connect each pair and fill in the missing letters, you'll eventually decipher the hidden word "**Lockers**"—the next location in the treasure hunt game.

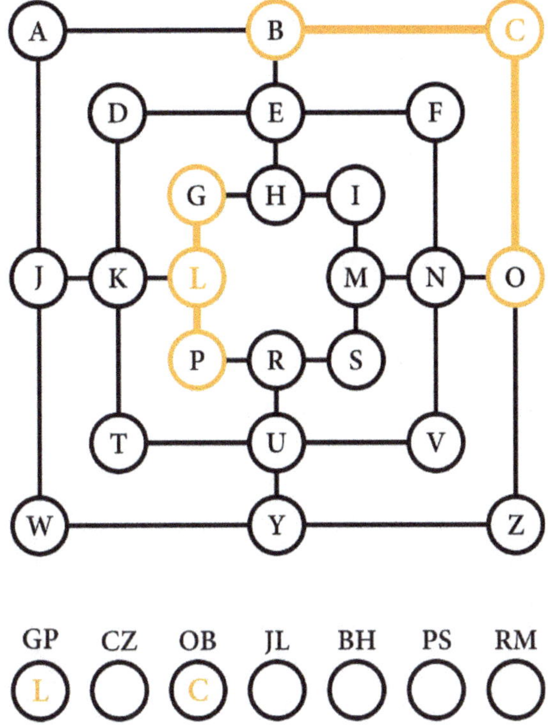

To simplify the cipher for the participants, you can design the board so that the letters in the corners are never used. However, this method takes a bit more effort, as you'll need to customise the board each time you create a new cipher.

CHAPTER 16
PLANNING PHASE

Now that you know how to create ciphers for your first hunt, it's time to discuss what you should consider when building your own game. Encrypting messages is one thing; putting them together logically to create an unforgettable game experience is another level entirely.

The start of any successful treasure hunt begins with the critical planning or brainstorming phase.

You can break down the initial phase into the following categories:

1. Route of the Treasure Hunt
2. Length of the Game
3. Number of Participants
4. Testing & Difficulty
5. Hints & Help
6. Finish & Wrap Up

Let's delve into these key areas one by one:

1. Route of the Treasure Hunt

You need to start with the location of the game in mind. Consider where the treasure hunt will take your participants before encrypting any locations in your ciphers. You can easily opt-in for an office space – that's a great idea! But can your office accommodate everyone, and is it large enough for a treasure hunt? These are crucial questions to ask yourself before creating ciphers. We'll dedicate a separate chapter to virtual treasure hunts, so this section will focus on physical spaces only.

If you continue with the office space as a place for your treasure hunt, consider the distance when deciding where to hide your clues. They shouldn't be too close together (adjacent meeting rooms) or too far apart (halfway across the city in a different office building). Ideally, it should take participants 1-5 minutes to get from one clue location to the next one.

This means it's absolutely fine to have two or three steps of your Treasure hunt on different sides of your office floor, but it also means you might need to spread the game across multiple office floors or the entire office building. This can present challenges, as you need to ensure that all clue steps are accessible to every participant.

All location steps should be in logical order. You shouldn't send people one direction and then ask them to come back immediately after. This means that if you have locations in the lobby, on the first floor, and some on the second floor, it's a good idea that the treasure hunt leads your participants to all locations on one floor before leading them to the next one.

This approach also prevents a situation where a team that's almost done suddenly meets a team that's halfway through the game. The other team might find a clue location that the first team is solving and think they are catching up. By putting clues in order logically, you ensure no teams get shortcuts during the treasure hunt.

When placing clues in the destined locations, make sure they are hidden but still findable. For example, if you place a clue in a meeting room, it should not be visible to someone who just walks in.

However, if someone knows to look for a clue there, they should be able to find it within 10-15 seconds. You could hide it under the table or behind something in the room. It should be easy to reach but not obvious to people who aren't part of the treasure hunt.

When planning your treasure hunt, always ask for

permission. If you want to put a clue in a lobby bar, ask the owner first. Make sure they know what's happening to avoid surprises. Tell them when people will come looking for clues and remove the clue after the game. This helps to keep everyone happy and maintains good relationships. Use the same approach when using public spaces for a treasure hunt. Make sure the clue is hidden well so only the players can find it. Be careful not to break any laws or rules. After the game, remove the clue to keep the area clean and safe for everyone.

2. Length of the Game

You don't want to make the activity too short or too long, so how many steps should you include? From my experience, the perfect treasure hunt has around 10 clue steps. This setup usually takes teams between 40 to 100 minutes of pure game time, with most teams finishing in about 70 minutes.

When creating a treasure hunt, I've found that 10 clues hit the sweet spot. This number allows players to flex their creativity, work together, mislead each other with different opinions on how to solve each riddle and explore different locations around the office or the city.

While adding more clues can be thrilling for teams that excel (believe me, the top teams always feel that the game is too short), it can also be too much for others. If the riddles are tough and some teams need a lot of help, they might get frustrated knowing they're only halfway through with many steps left to solve. In these cases, they might even consider giving up. Keeping a reasonable number of steps in the treasure hunt can help prevent this.

When you're planning, don't forget to factor in time for introductions and a wrap-up. I recommend setting aside at least two hours for the entire activity (15-20 minutes for introduction, 90 minutes for the game time and 15-20 minutes for evaluation and debriefing). No one minds finishing early, but it's not ideal to cut the event short. If you're hesitant about whether everyone will enjoy a full treasure hunt or if you don't have so much time, you can try to start small. You can create a five-step version first. This shorter hunt can be done in about an hour, including introductions and debriefing, though top teams might finish in just 15-20 minutes of playtime (but the majority should take around 35 minutes). This approach allows you to test the waters and gather feedback before planning a longer treasure hunt in the future.

But why does this publication include 15 ciphers when I recommend creating a treasure hunt with only 10 steps?

From my experience, having a variety of ciphers provides more flexibility and keeps things interesting. You might find that you enjoy some ciphers more than others. Use the ones you like the most or feel confident recreating.

Additionally, having extra ciphers allows you to introduce fresh challenges in your future treasure hunts, keeping the experience new and exciting even for those who participated in your first game. It's perfectly fine to reuse some clue steps from previous events, especially if you encrypt a different message.

3. Number of Participants

In your planning phase, think about how many people will play. The approach you choose will differ based on the number of participants.

If you have 10-15 people in 2-3 teams, they can easily fit into the office space/restaurant/bar/insert your area where you'll play the game. When only a couple of people are involved, it usually doesn't create too much chaos, and it's hardly noticeable if someone sees a group of people around a meeting room trying to solve their cipher.

Smaller numbers of participants can easily fit indoors as they can search for clues and solve them directly on the spot or very nearby without causing a "traffic jam." However, if you have 100+ people, the office space might get too crowded. Check if the location can handle all of your participants. If it can, great! Use that spot. But if you are sending more than a hundred people to a small place at once, it's usually not a good idea.

Having many small locations one after another won't work well either. So, before organising a company-wide treasure hunt for hundreds of employees in your office space, consider using an outdoor setup instead.

At the start of a treasure hunt, many teams solve clues at similar times. This means that you will have multiple teams together in the first few locations. These early steps need to handle large groups of people together. As the treasure hunt goes on, teams will spread out. Some teams will solve clues quickly, while others take more time. By the sixth or seventh location, there won't be as many people trying to solve the same clue at once.

To plan your space, utilise large areas such as communal spaces, building lobby, event spaces, and canteens at the beginning of the game. Later in the hunt, you can use smaller spaces like meeting rooms, call booths, and kitchen areas since fewer people will be there at the same time.

These suggestions usually apply only to bigger treasure hunts consisting of 40 or more participants. If you plan something smaller, maybe a game just for your teammates, then you can use smaller spaces, and the physical distance between different steps can be much shorter.

4. Testing & Difficulty

Once you start creating your treasure hunt ciphers, account for some time for testing and possible adjustments to the difficulty of your game. It's extremely important to have someone test the ciphers you created.

I've made the mistake of thinking I didn't need help because I was confident in my work, that I did the same cipher million times. But on the day of the treasure hunt, to my disbelief, participants struggled with a clue that could have been easily fixed, if someone else had tested it.

Unfortunate mistakes and extreme difficulty of certain ciphers create bad experience for the people and leave a bitter mark. Good news is that this can be very easily prevented.

Ask someone to test your ciphers to ensure that everything can be deciphered correctly and logically. If you do this with them in person, you will also see how long it takes your participants (or, in this case, a person who is being your tester) to solve your riddles and if and where they get stuck. It will give you the immediate opportunity to adjust the difficulty by providing a hint. If the hint doesn't help, you can always rework the cipher using an easier encryption method.

It's okay for participants to ask for one or two hints in a 10-step treasure hunt. It means it's challenging but not impossible. However, if they need help at almost every step, it means the design is too difficult and not fun.

Participants may feel frustrated and not smart enough, which ruins their experience. Remember, you're creating this for everyday Joe's, not for professionals. There is a big chance your participants might not have done a treasure hunt before, so bear that in mind.

I highly recommend watching the tester play your treasure hunt to fully understand its difficulty level. They don't need to go through the physical locations; it is enough to watch them solve the riddles. Just ask a colleague or a friend—it's a fun activity that you can do over a lunch break or after work while having a beer.

It's even better if you include someone who will miss out the treasure hunt on the day—this way you'll make sure they feel included, valued and they won't have a fear of missing out. And you get the best feedback in return. Perfect win-win situation.

5. Hints & Help

Hints are essential to keep participants on the right track. If someone struggles with a clue for more than five or seven minutes without making progress, they might lose interest in the game and give up. The goal of the organiser should be to help everyone to finish their game.

Offering hints & giving help can keep attendees motivated and on track. Here are three effective ways to provide hints:

Name the Cipher: Give your cipher a name that includes a hint. You can play with fonts and stylistics of the name, e.g. using words in bold or capital letters to highlight the key focus.

For example, we can name the flag cipher "Big City Life" referencing both the popular song and the fact, that we should look at cities, not at the countries.

Add a Pictogram: A small picture can offer significant guidance, drawing attention to the key elements.

Let's continue with the example of Flag cipher. Now a picture in the background can immediately hint that the focus should be on a capital city, rather than a country.

Use a Description: A brief description can guide participants on what to focus on without giving away the answer. Using the same example, a description hint to the flag cipher can be: *"Flag is only the first layer. You need to guess more than a country to get the capital solution."*

Make sure your hints are clear and not confusing. Their goal is to help and not to mislead people. Avoid adding anything that could make them more lost or frustrated. You can decide whether to provide a hint with every clue or reserve hints for the more challenging ones. You'll get a better sense of which clues might need hints after having them tested by someone.

But sometimes, even with all the hints, participants can get stuck, and they don't know what to do next. So, what should they do if they're stuck? Should they give up? Of course not! Everyone wants to finish and have fun. When people need help during a treasure hunt, you should have a plan.

What works for me is creating a helpline. As an organiser, I include my phone number for all the treasure hunts I run. This works well if there are fewer than 100 attendees. If there are more, you might need more people on the hotline. You can split the help between different teams.

I usually tell the participants, that if they're stuck on a clue for more than five or six minutes, they should call me. They shouldn't be afraid to call; it's better to move on and enjoy the game. Some teams might wait 10 or 15 minutes before calling because they are stubborn and they want to find the solution only by themselves, and that's okay, too. When I get a call from a team needing my assistance, I ask for their team name and who's solving the clue with them. I also ask where they are in the treasure hunt to identify where they need my help, and I ask them what methods they've tried so far (this gives me great feedback for future games).

I wouldn't recommend giving exact answer when someone asks for help. I tend to guide them towards the right solution without giving away the answer. It's more fun for them if they still have to solve the clue after my help. A short 1-minute phone call is usually enough to help them move on. Just stay by your phone and be ready to assist.

What about other forms of help besides a phone call? Could you use chat or a company internal messaging tool? From my experience, I wouldn't recommend using messaging as a helpline. When your teams need help, it's urgent. Messaging can be slow and inefficient in these situations. It takes time for them to write out their issue, for you to read it, and then to ask follow-up questions. Something that could be resolved in a minute over the phone might take five minutes over chat. And that's only if you notice the message right away, which can be tricky during the rush of the game.

If you're hosting a treasure hunt outdoors where phone reception isn't ideal, I suggest setting up a designated help point and communicating its location in advance. That way, if teams need assistance, they'll know exactly where to find you.

6. Finish & Wrap Up

As a final step, create an exciting conclusion for the treasure hunt with a clear finish line. Just like in any race, the finish line should be clear and celebrated, not a confusing afterthought. Imagine running a marathon and not realising you've crossed the finish line until much later—that would be disappointing. Your participants need to feel the thrill of nearing the end and the satisfaction of completing the hunt at the right moment.

For a physical finish, set up a leaderboard where participants can sign their team names and record their times upon arrival. For a virtual finish, provide a web-link where teams can enter their names and view their rankings in real-time (a simple live Google sheet document is enough, but you can also opt in for more elegant solutions).

Select a finish location spacious enough for all participants to gather, debrief, and celebrate. Ensure there's ample room for everyone to chat, relax, and share their experiences. Usually, you can reuse the same location that you've used for a start—it will create a nice loop.

Wrap up the event by announcing the winners and distributing any prizes (optional, but highly recommended). Conclude the treasure hunt with everyone together, sharing final announcements and next steps and enjoying the atmosphere.

As an organiser, don't forget to ask for feedback when it's fresh. Talk to people to find out what they liked about your game and what could be improved. Ask for ciphers where people struggled and find out if any riddles were too easy. These insights will help you make your next game even better.

CHAPTER 17
VIRTUAL TREASURE HUNT

In some ways, a virtual treasure hunt is a bit easier to organise.

While an in-person treasure hunt is ideal for creating those Indiana Jones like memories when discovering different clue step locations, a virtual game can be an excellent alternative, especially for teams spread across different locations and timezones. Virtual treasure hunts also offer fantastic opportunities for collaboration and team bonding.

One major advantage of a virtual game is the absence of physical space constraints, making the setup much quicker. You don't need to plan a physical route, and with the same number of ciphers, the game progresses faster since participants don't need to travel between locations.

There are many ways to create and run a virtual treasure hunt, and I've found my own approach through trial and error. What I'll share here is just how I do it, but there's no right way—you can adapt these steps to fit your own style.

Personally, I like to keep things simple. In my experience, technology and software can be unpredictable, especially when you least expect it—like a shaky internet connection or not being able to share your screen at a crucial moment. That's why I always aim to make the virtual game as foolproof as possible. Even if something goes wrong on my end, participants can still stay engaged and complete the game without interruptions. Here's how to get started:

Create Your Ciphers
Design your ciphers just like you normally would, but

instead of printing them, save them as PDFs and upload them to a platform that everyone can easily access. Google Drive, SharePoint, Slack, or even Discord work great for this. Make sure to organise the files in the correct order, naming them something simple and clear, like "Cipher 1" or "Step 1," followed by "Cipher 2" / "Step 2" and so on.

Lock the Ciphers Using Passcode

The first cipher should be an unlocked PDF that participants can open immediately. From there, every subsequent cipher should be password-protected. This means, that when the game starts, participants must solve the first cipher to obtain the password for the next PDF. For example, solving "Cipher 1" provides the password to unlock "Cipher 2," and solving "Cipher 2" provides the password for "Cipher 3," and so on.

Choose a consistent format for all your passwords and stick with it. I recommend using all lowercase letters without spaces if your password has multiple words. A good example would be using "treasurehunt" instead of "TREASURE HUNT". At the start of the game communicate the password format to the participants to prevent any misunderstandings.

Locking your PDF files with a password is quite easy. Just open the PDF, go to the permissions or security settings, typically found under the "File" or "Edit" menu and choose the option to add a password. Enter your password and save the file. The steps might be a bit different on Windows and MacOS, but you shouldn't need any additional software to lock your ciphers. If you get stuck, a quick Google search will bring up plenty of guides to help you out.

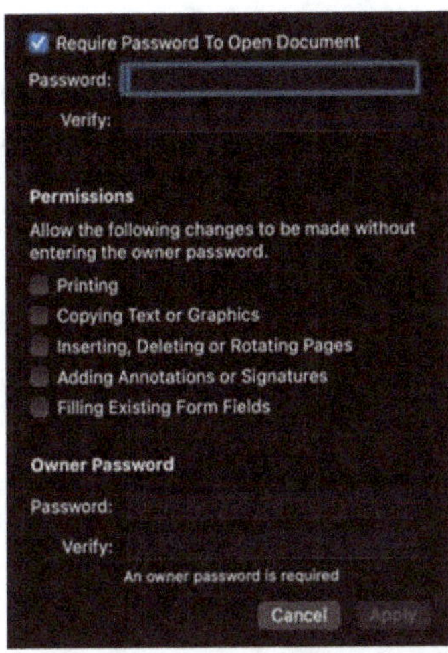

Most mistakes tend to happen when locking your PDFs, so double-check everything. Make sure you're entering the correct passwords—the solution to "Clue 1" is the password for "Clue 2" PDF, and so on. Take a moment to test opening each file with the corresponding password to ensure everything works. This simple step can save you and your participants a lot of frustration during the virtual game.

Video Conferencing Platform

The only other thing you need for a virtual treasure hunt is a video conferencing platform that can accommodate all participants. Use Zoom / Webex / Teams or anything else you have access to or use internally. When everyone joins, start by explaining the rules and provide instructions (we'll cover this in the next chapter). I always provide my phone number as a backup so teams can still reach me for help if the videoconferencing fails. It's a safety net I hope not to use, but it's important to have just in case.

Once you're ready to start, divide the teams into virtual breakout rooms so they can collaborate independently. If they need help, they can easily return to the main room at any point to ask for help. At the end of the game, bring everyone back to the main room for a wrap-up, debrief and feedback.

If that feels too complex, another option is to host just one call where you explain the rules and start the game. Once it's underway, each team can leave the main call and set up their own for the treasure hunt. If anyone needs help during the game, they can always come back to the original call, where you'll be available to offer hints as needed.

To make the experience more personal, I strongly encourage all participants to keep their video on throughout the whole game, especially when the game starts and participants are in their small breakout rooms. This way, they can interact with faces rather than with blank screens. This small step is very important for the overall mood and usually improves how participants feel throughout and after the game. Even if they're remote, they can get to know each other better this way.

It's also incredibly helpful if one participant shares their screen, allowing the entire team to follow along as they work through the clues. This practice ensures that everyone stays on the same page and remains fully engaged.

The goal is for the whole group to collaborate on deciphering each step together, rather than having individuals try to solve the riddle on their own and the first person who figures it out simply share the answer. When teams work together, everyone can follow the process and stay fully engaged throughout the virtual game, making the experience much more enjoyable for all.

CHAPTER 18
PREPARATION ON THE DAY

Now that we've covered the planning phase of the treasure hunt let's talk about what you'll need on the day of the event. By now, you should have all your clues and riddles ready, and you've planned the route, duration, and number of participants.

On the day of the treasure hunt, a working printer will be your best friend. Print all the clues you'll place at each location. Half of an A4 page (A5 format) is sufficient. Print each clue twice in case one gets damaged and needs replacing.

In some games, you can print every step for every team and instruct all teams to take one copy of the clue they need to solve. This is the easiest way for teams to physically touch and solve the clues. However, from my experience, one clue for everyone is sufficient. Simply instruct all teams to take a picture of the clue and leave it intact.

This method allows hundreds of people to participate without any issues, and it is also the most environmentally friendly way to set up your game.

You'll also need scissors and tape. Head to all the locations about an hour or two before the game starts. Tape each clue at the location someplace where it's not too visible, but that still can be found easily by participants. Ensure you place them correctly to avoid any mix-ups that could disrupt the game. This is where most mistakes can happen, so be precise! Placing a different clue at the wrong location will disrupt the entire game, so be careful and double-check that you're putting the right clue in the right place. This process involves visiting each location and carefully attaching or hanging up the clues in the correct order.

If you have the time (or if you have someone to help), visit each location once more just before the game starts to ensure everything is still in place.

Team Division & Team Dynamics

Before the treasure hunt begins, divide everyone into teams. For a virtual treasure hunt, use simple tools like Google Forms or Microsoft Forms for sign-ups. For in-person games, you can use a whiteboard and let people create their own teams.

Teams should consist of 4 to 6 people. Having more than six members makes it difficult for everyone to discuss clues and collaborate effectively. In larger groups, dominant personalities tend to take control, leaving shy or less outspoken individuals with less opportunity to participate. While four-five person teams are ideal, six person teams are also manageable (especially for in-person games).

Avoid teams with 3 and less people, as this can be too challenging and less enjoyable. The game is designed to create bonds and memories, to get to know other people you rarely work with, to introduce new-hires to the teams and hence, it should not be played solo or in very small teams.

You can also set up specific criteria if you want to mix people from different teams and departments. For example, you can establish a rule that a maximum of two people from the same department can be in a team together. This way, you can mix members from sales, marketing, product, and legal departments, consciously creating space for cross-department collaboration.

That said, this approach might take away some of the fun for departments who enjoy playing together or even competing against each other. The final decision really depends on the outcome you're aiming for. If the goal is purely to have fun, let people choose their own teams. But if you'd like certain departments to work more closely together, you can adjust the sign-up process to reflect that.

Be sure to communicate the team size rules clearly before the game begins. You could set up a sign-up sheet on a whiteboard with markers so people can join teams throughout the day. The more teams you have organised ahead of time, the more smoothly things will run once the game starts.

Of course, even with the best planning, there will always be a few shy participants or last-minute arrivals without a team. Handle these situations quickly by assigning them to existing teams or, if needed, creating new teams on the spot. Encourage early sign-ups, or make sure there's enough time for team creation before you dive into explaining the rules and kicking off the game.

Team Supplies

Ensure each team is equipped with some basic supplies. Every team will need a notepad or a few pieces of paper and some pens or pencils. These items are essential for solving the clues and riddles you have prepared. The key is to ensure they have tools to test their ideas and figure out the solutions. Prepare these bundles ahead of time for every team. Additionally, you can print out instructions and distribute them along with the pens and paper. Include your phone number or another way for teams to get help if they get stuck during the game. Here's a checklist to ensure you cover everything:

Pen & Paper: To note down ideas, clues and possible answers, make sure that everyone has access to pens, pencils and paper.
Instructions: Print out a set of instructions for each team detailing the game rules and objectives.
Contact Information: Include your phone number or another method for teams to reach out if they need help.

Explain the Rules

As a last step before starting the game, gather everyone and explain the rules clearly. Inform them that this is a treasure hunt game consisting of 10 riddles (or as many steps as you have planned). When they solve the first riddle, it will direct them to a new location, and every consecutive solution will lead them to the next one. All team members should always move together to find another cipher. This process will continue until they reach the last location. After solving the tenth riddle, they will be guided to the finish line.

If you've got rewards lined up, you can either announce the prizes (and how many teams will win) or keep it as a secret surprise. Just ensure everyone understands the basic rules of the game. Internet use is generally allowed, as it won't provide any significant advantage, so there is no need to prohibit It.

Allocate a few moments for questions (and prepare to answer those as there will be a few) before the game starts, allowing teams to clarify any uncertainties.

Emphasise the importance of staying together as a team at all times. It's crucial for fun and fairness that no one splits up. Also, mention that there are no trick locations; each clue will clearly indicate the next destination, so there's no need for teams to split up and visit multiple locations simultaneously In hopes of finding the right place quickly. As an example, If a clue will lead participants to a meeting room, It will clearly specify Ih meeting room should the team visit.

Before the game begins, provide each team with a printed copy of the first clue along with their supply bundle. Instruct them not to look at it until you officially start the game. You can give them the paper upside down or in an envelope to prevent peeking. Once everyone is ready, tell them to open it and start deciphering the first clue. Alternatively, you can reveal the first clue and let teams come closer to take a picture of it before they start solving it.

This Is it! Congratulations on launching the first treasure hunt. You've done an amazing job.

Example of Printed Instructions:

Hey everyone!

Please don't open the first clue before we start! There are 10 ciphers in total—you've got the first one in your hand and nine more to find. The first team to reach the end wins the treasure.

The first clue takes place right here in our event space. Before we get going, find a spot for you and your team, and try to spread out so the other teams can't peek over your shoulders. But don't wander too far—if you haven't solved the first clue after 7 minutes, we'll give a hint to everyone.

*If you're stuck on a clue for a while (more than 5 minutes) and have no idea what to do, give us a call at **+44 77XX XXXXXX** for a hint.*

All the clues are indoors in places you can get to with your office badge. If you're sure you're in the right spot and still can't find the clue, call the helpline. Usually, the simplest solution is the right one, so don't overthink it. Make sure your whole team sticks together and goes to each place as a group!

There's only one clue at each location. Please don't take it off the wall, mess with it, or touch it. Just take a picture of the cipher and figure it out together. Bring a pen or pencil and some paper—it'll help you solve the clues faster if you can jot down notes.

Good luck and have fun, hunters!

During the Game

As teams begin solving their clues, stay at the first location to assist the slower teams. Offer hints after about 5-7 minutes to ensure everyone can move from the first step to the next. Once everyone has moved to the second location, you can decide to either stay at the back with the slower teams or move freely between multiple locations. Since you know all the spots, but the participants don't, you can check in on each team's progress and take some pictures.

Get ready for helpline calls, especially as the game goes on. The deeper into the game, the more calls you'll get. So, keep your phone handy and be prepared to offer hints and guidance to keep everyone moving along. Walk with the teams and observe how they're doing for about 30 to 40 minutes.

After this initial period, locate the leading team and stick with them so you can be at the finish line when they arrive. It's important to be there to celebrate with the first team. Congratulate them and help them log their finish time on the leaderboard. This way, all teams can compare their times and see how they performed compared to others.

Debrief & Evaluation

There will be a notable time difference between the first and last team, sometimes even longer than 30 minutes, so it's unreasonable to ask everyone to wait around patiently. To keep the atmosphere fun and engaging, make sure the teams that have already finished have something to do. You could organise a coffee break or offer drinks and snacks to maintain a good mood while waiting for the others to finish.

Once all the teams have crossed the finish line, you can hold the evaluation session. Announce the winners and share the results. If you've prepared prizes for the winning teams, now's the prefect time to hand them over, congratulate the winners and capture the moment with a few photos to commemorate the occasion. You can reveal the average time it took for teams to complete the hunt, as well as the times for the third place, second place, and winning teams. This not only highlights the achievements but also adds an extra layer of excitement and competition to the event.

During this debrief, encourage teams to share their experiences, what they enjoyed, what did they learn about each other and what challenges they faced. This isn't just about reliving the fun moments, it's also an opportunity to reinforce the objectives you've set for the team-building.

Last but not least, don't forget to ask for feedback on the game and ciphers you've created. This feedback is invaluable for improving future treasure hunts. It's also a great way to wrap up the event on a positive note, celebrating everyone's efforts and creating lasting memories.

CHAPTER 19
NAVIGATING THE ROUGH PATCHES

I won't sugarcoat it—sometimes, things don't go according to plan, and hiccups can happen during a treasure hunt. When things go wrong, it can take away some of the fun. But don't worry, I've been there, and with a little preparation, you can avoid most of these bumps in the road. Here, I'll share some common mistakes people make and give you practical tips to steer clear of them.

First and foremost, remember that people are here to have fun, and they'll appreciate the effort you've put in. Most folks will forgive small hiccups along the way, so don't be too hard on yourself. Now, let's talk about the most common issues:

Time Management

Time management is one of the biggest challenges not only in everyday life but also during the treasure hunt. You might think everything is perfectly planned, but trust me, things often take longer than expected. Whether it's explaining the rules or letting teams settle in, time slips away faster than you realise. My advice? Plan for more time than you think you'll need. For example, if you're running a 10-cipher treasure hunt, schedule at least two hours and tack on an extra 30 minutes as a buffer. This way, you won't end up rushing through the end, and teams can enjoy the experience without feeling pressed for time.

Difficult and Incorrect Ciphers

This is by far one of the most common, but also one of the easiest mistakes to avoid. Testing is the key!

Always, always test your hunt with someone who hasn't seen the ciphers before. It's like a dress rehearsal, helping you catch mistakes and make sure the game is both fun and straightforward. This also gives you a sense of how difficult the ciphers are—trust me; there's nothing worse than spending the entire game on the phone, explaining how to solve puzzles to every single team. Adjust the difficulty based on feedback so that it's challenging, but not frustrating. It's all about the right balance!

Despite all the testing, if you find yourself in a situation where a cipher is unsolvable due to an error you didn't spot before, don't panic. The best thing to do is cut your losses and step in. Head to the location tied to the incorrect cipher and give the players the solution so they know where to go next.

Missing or Removed Ciphers

Every now and then, a cipher disappears, and often it's a genuine accident. Maybe someone wiped it off the whiteboard while tidying up the meeting room or mistakenly took it without realizing its importance. But there are also cases where people intentionally remove or hide a cipher, either to mess with the game or to gain an unfair advantage. Unfortunately, this kind of behaviour can throw the whole hunt off course and ruin the fun for others.

In an outdoor setup, weather can also play a role. A cipher could get blown away by the wind or destroyed by unexpected rain, and as the organiser, you just have to be ready for that! If a team can't find the next clue, they're stuck and can't continue. To avoid this, always print two copies of each cipher. That way, if a team calls in saying they can't find a clue, you can confirm their location and quickly replace the missing one without derailing the game.

Distractions

Distractions can be a game killer. Before you even start planning the game, it's important to check in with your participants and make sure there aren't any big meetings, deadlines, or other obligations pulling at their attention. People multitasking during a treasure hunt often don't have as much fun because their mind isn't fully in the game. And really, the whole point of this is to create an experience where everyone can focus, bond, and have fun together.

External factors can be just as disruptive. Another event at the same venue, could easily pull focus away from your game. Noise, large crowds, or simply the curiosity of what's happening next door can dilute the fun, So, do a quick check to avoid detracting factors.

Cheating or Rule-bending

Ah, cheating. It happens even in team-building treasure hunts, though often not in the way you'd expect. Most of the time, people cheat without even realising it! You might be wondering how that's possible. Well, sometimes, a team wrongly decrypts a clue or guesses the wrong location.

Then by sheer luck, they end up somewhere they weren't supposed to be yet—maybe they stumble upon another team or find a clue meant for later in the game. They think they're right on track, but they've actually skipped a few steps. This kind of "unknowing" cheating happens more often than you'd think.

In these cases, I usually don't sweat it. As long as the teams are having fun and they don't accidentally cheat their way into the top 3, I just laugh it off. I'll often ask them if they want to go back and solve the ciphers they skipped, and it's usually all in good spirits.

But then, of course, there's intentional cheating. This can happen when there's a tempting reward at stake. Some players might decide to follow another team, figuring they can skip the problem-solving part altogether. It doesn't usually happen right away, but as the excitement builds and the competition heats up, and the temptation to cut corners grows. To minimise cheating, one easy trick is to ask teams for evidence when they complete the treasure hunt. For example, have them take photos of each cipher at its correct location. This simple request works wonders for keeping things honest.

You can also quiz teams at the end—ask how they solved certain ciphers and what their thought process was. It's a good way to check if they've genuinely worked through all the clues and locations. By asking for this kind of evidence, you can ensure the game stays fair when announcing results.

Wrapping It Up

While it might feel like a lot could go wrong, don't let that intimidate you. The reality is, these little bumps along the way are part of the fun! Most of the potential issues are easy to fix, and with just a bit of planning, you can prevent most of them before they even arise.

In the end, the goal is simple: for everyone to have a great time. So, approach it with a positive attitude, embrace any surprises, and remember to keep the focus on having fun.

FINAL THOUGHTS FROM THE AUTHOR

Now it's your turn to become the game master. I hope this guide has given you the confidence and inspiration to create your own treasure hunt. If the idea of organising a big event feels a bit overwhelming, don't worry—starting small is a great way to ease into it. Try putting together 4-5 riddles and inviting a friend or colleague to test them out. Their reactions will give you valuable insights, help you fine-tune your clues, and boost your confidence.

In my experience, people absolutely love the thrill of solving riddles and genuinely appreciate the effort you've put into crafting such an engaging experience. The best part? You don't need a huge budget—what really matters is the time, creativity, and thoughtfulness you pour into it.

Creating each clue might take 30 to 60 minutes, and you'll need a few more hours to piece together the route, prepare all the materials, and print out the instructions. All in all, you can expect to spend around 6+ hours bringing your treasure hunt to life. While many companies choose to outsource this to team-building agencies if they have the budget, with the knowledge you've gained here, you're fully equipped to create an amazing team-building experience on your own.

Thank you for trusting me to be part of your next team-building adventure. I hope these ideas and tips help you create an unforgettable experience for your team. If you ever need more guidance or want to share feedback, I'd love to hear from you; feel free to reach out through LinkedIn, or social media channels. Let's keep building amazing moments together!

www.ingramcontent.com/pod-product-compliance
Lightning Source LLC
LaVergne TN
LVHW010456200726

843506LV00002B/129